Contents

1. Shapes

A Words to Know

Highlight the words you know.

Target Words

shapes	circle	cone	cylinder	diamond
hexagon	line	oval	pentagon	rectangle
square	star	triangle		

B A Day at the Circus

See lots of shapes. Look and write.

1. _ _ _ _ ang _ _

2. s _ _ _

3. s _ _ _ _ e

4. _ _ _ an _ _ e

5. _ _ _ _ le

6. o _ _ _

7. p _ _ t _ _ _ _

C Half Shapes

Complete the pictures. Look and write.

1.

2.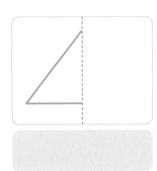

3.

4.

5.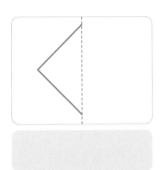

6.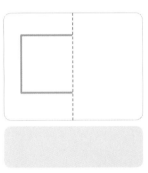

D Word Split

Connect each picture to the right word. Match and trace.

1.

2.

3.

4.

cyl   co   penta   hex

 gon    agon   inder   ne

E Word Maze

Follow the shapes and write the words.

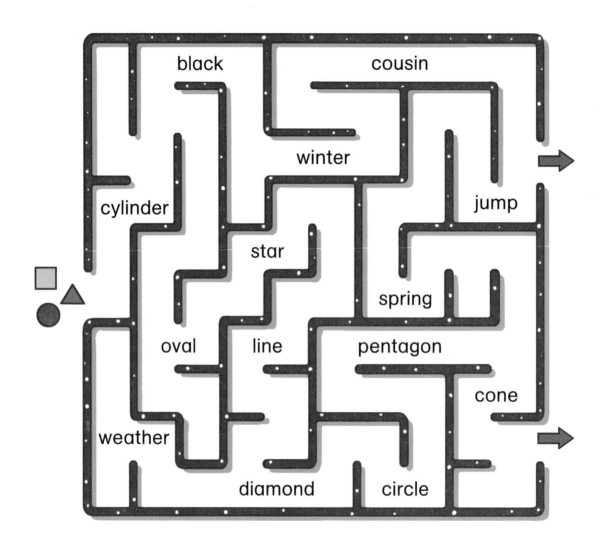

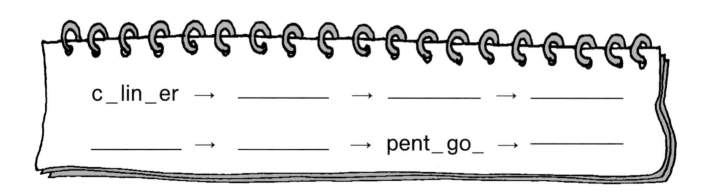

c_lin_er → _____ → _____ → _____

_____ → _____ → pent_go_ → _____

He sees a **circle** this time.

He peeks inside and sees a **star**.

A What Does He See?

Bobby sees many different shapes in the box. Look and write.

1.

He sees
a sq_____.

2.

He sees
a _____ this time.

3.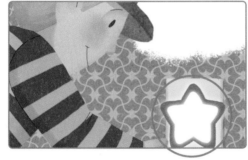

He peeks inside and
sees a _____.

4.

He finally sees
a r_____.

B Write Right!

Unscramble and write.

| and | a star. | sees | peeks inside | He |

 **2. Toys**

A Words to Know

Highlight the words you know.

Target Words

toys	block	card	checkers	clay
dice	doll	jump rope	kite	marble
puzzle	robot	slingshot		

B New Toy Store!

See these wonderful toys. Look and write.

1. d _ _ _

2. _ o _ o _

3. _ _ o _ _

4. ju _ _ r _ p _

5. _ _ t _

6. _ _ _ l

C Messy Room

Put all the toys back to the shelf. Unscramble, write, and number.

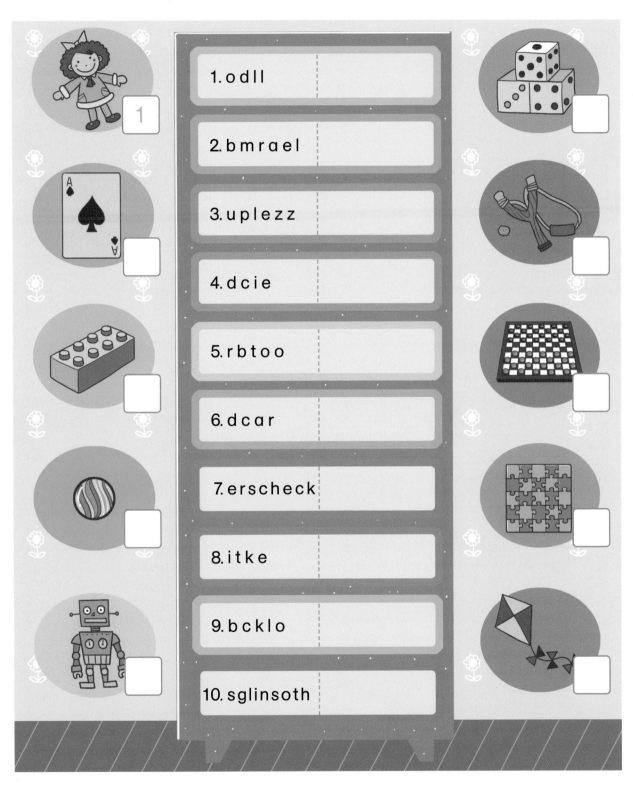

1. o d l l
2. b m r a e l
3. u p l e z z
4. d c i e
5. r b t o o
6. d c a r
7. e r s c h e c k
8. i t k e
9. b c k l o
10. s g l i n s o t h

D Ladder Search

Take the toys down the ladders. Follow and write twice.

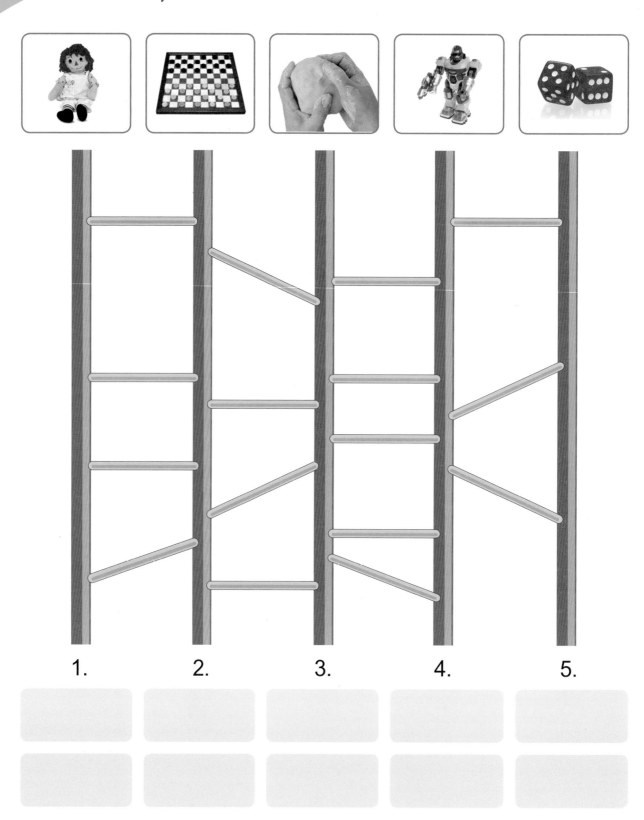

1.

2.

3.

4.

5.

Is this a puzzle?

Yes, it is.

 A **A Nice Surprise**

Bobby gets a surprise present. Read and write.

What else is in the box? Bobby sees a triangle.

"Is this a puzzle?" asks Bobby.

"Yes, it is." says Dad. Bobby likes the animal puzzle.

It looks like a lot of fun!

1.

2.

 B **Read Again!**

Complete the dialogue.

 "Is this a _____?"

 " _____, it is."

Review

Day 5

A Shape Hunt

Look at the frames. Look and count.

1. circle ☐

2. square ☐

3. rectangle ☐

4. triangle ☐

5. hexagon ☐

B Math Game

Find the words that match the pictures.
Do the math and write them.

1.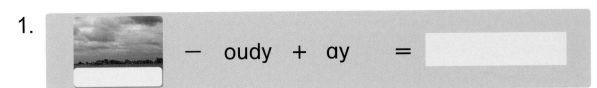

   — oudy + ay =

2.

   d + [bowl] — r =

3.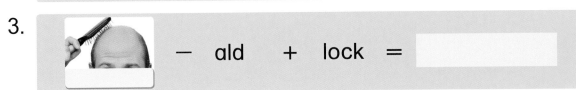

   — ald + lock =

Word Bank

cloudy   bald   rice

C Shape Stories

Read and guess the missing words. Find and write.

1.

Today is my birthday.
Look at all the _____
of the gifts. How exciting!

2.

Bobby looks inside the box.
He sees a _____.
It's his favorite peanut
cookie!

3.

"I love your b_____s,
_____s, cards,
and games," Lisa says.

Word Bank

doll   circle   shapes   block

3. Farm Animals

A Words to Know

Highlight the words you know.

Target Words

farm animals	cat	cow	dog	duck
frog	goat	hen	horse	pig
rabbit	rooster	sheep		

B A New Day at the Farm

Visit a friendly farm. Look and write.

1. _ oo _ _ _ _

2. h _ _ _ e

3. _ u _ _

4. c _ _

5. _ _ g

6. sh _ _ p

7. _ _ bb _ _

C Pigpen

Help the animals out of the mud. Unscramble and write.

1. r f o g

_____ ☐

2. s e e h p

_____ ☐

3. g i p

_____ ☐

4. d c k u

_____ ☐

5. d g o

_____ ☐

6. r s t o o r e

_____ ☐

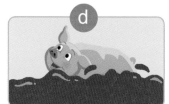

a

b

c

d

e

f

D Animal House

Look at his house. Look and write.

There are a cow,

a _____,

a _____, and

a _____ in his house.

Break the code to find 6 animals. Find and write.

□	●	★	▦	♤	◑	△	♫	♥	▣	◆	♨	♩	▨	♣
b	t	a	o	d	h	p	g	s	c	e	n	r	i	u

1. ▣ ★ ●

_____

2. △ ▨ ♫

_____

3. ♫ ▦ ★ ●

_____

4. ◑ ◆ ♨

_____

5. ♩ ▦ ▦ ♥ ● ◆ ♩

_____

6. ♩ ★ □ □ ▨ ●

_____

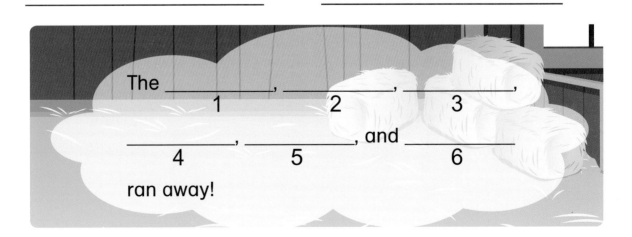

The _____, _____, _____,
     1   2   3

_____, _____, and _____
  4   5   6

ran away!

Go get a cow and a horse.

 A **Animal Problems**

A man wants to solve his problem. Read and circle the farm animals.

What's
your problem?

I can't sleep at night. My house is too noisy.

Go get a cow
and a horse.

What?
That sounds silly.

 B **Write Right!**

Unscramble and write.

and   Go   a horse.   get a cow

_____

4. Zoo Animals

A Words to Know

Highlight the words you know.

Target Words

zoo animals		bear	deer	dolphin
elephant	fox	giraffe	kangaroo	lion
monkey	owl	snake	tiger	turtle
whale	wolf	zebra		

B A Day at the Zoo

Visit the zoo. Look and write.

1. b _ _ r

2. _ _ _ ra

3. l _ _ _

4. _ _ ra _ _ _

5. _ ur _ _ _

6. sn _ _ _

7. _ l _ _ h _ _ t

C Letter to Letter

Look at the scattered letters. Connect and write twice.

1.

b i a n

l e o r

bear

_____

_____

2.

d h u b

r e e r

_____

_____

3.

t a g x r

k i b e d

_____

_____

4.

f o a k w

s n n x e

_____

_____

5.

g e b l a

z o w r j

_____

_____

6.

y n a l s

w h m c e

_____

_____

D Animal Riddles

Guess what is described. Find and write.

1.
It crawls very slowly.
It has a thick shell.

_____

2.
It loves bananas.
It has a long tail.

_____

3.
It carries its baby.
It hops around.

_____

4.
It has a long neck.
It is very tall.

_____

5.
It has a long nose.
It has two strong tusks.

_____

6.
It has two wings.
It hunts at night.

_____

Word Bank

turtle	monkey	giraffe
kangaroo	owl	elephant

Words in Use

Look at the huge elephant!
Look at the funny monkey!

A Whose Line Is It?

Robin's family is having fun at the zoo. Find and write.

1.

Look at _____

_____!

2.

Look at _____

_____!

Word Bank

the funny monkey   the huge elephant

B Write Right!

Unscramble and write.

the   huge   elephant!   Look at

A Animal Homes

Look at the farm and zoo animals. Group and write.

1.

2.

B Animal Concert

Look at the outdoor concert. Look and write.

Look! The bird is playing the cello. The 1. _____ is playing the violin. The 2. _____ is playing the guitar. And the 3. _____ is playing the flute.

C Animal Stories

Find the matching pictures. Read, match, and trace.

1.

My dog makes
me smile.

a

2.

"Go get
a chicken and
a goat."

b

3.

"I was scared
of that bear!"

c

4.

The elephant
was very sad.

d

5. Body Parts

A Words to Know

Highlight the words you know.

Target Words

body	head	face	eye	nose
mouth	ear	hair	neck	shoulder
arm	hand	finger	leg	foot
feel	hear	look	see	smell

B My Body

Name each part of my body. Look and write.

1. _ y _

8. _ _ _ _ ld _ _

2. n _ _ _

7. m _ _ th

3. _ _ r

6. _ _ m

4. l _ _

5. f _ _ t

C Our Senses

Read what you can do with your body. Match and write.

1.  • • hear • • **a** I can hear with my _____s.

2.  • • see • • **b** I can see with my _____s.

3. 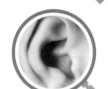 • • smell • • **c** I can feel with my _____s.

4.  • • feel • • **d** I can smell with my _____.

D Angry Letters

Calm down the letters. Unscramble and write twice.

1. a f c e _____ _____

2. c n e k _____ _____

3. r i n f g e _____ _____

4. t m h u o _____ _____

5. e u s r d o h l _____ _____

E Word Search

Circle the words. Find the pictures and write.

```
f  v  a  r  m  c  x  z  t  s
o  i  p  c  w  e  h  a  i  r
o  s  n  e  p  d  e  y  x  m
t  n  a  g  l  u  a  j  w  o
o  o  x  v  e  p  d  u  g  u
y  s  b  n  g  r  v  b  n  t
u  e  t  p  y  f  o  i  r  h
```

1.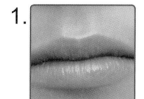

_ _ _ th

2.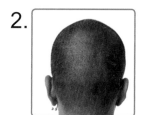

h _ _ _

3.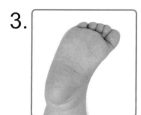

f _ _ t

4.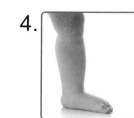

_ e _

5.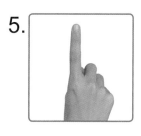

f _ _ g _ _

6.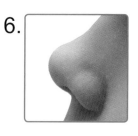

_ o _ _

7.

_ _ m

8.

_ a _ _

I want long legs like Dad.

A Growing Up

Vinnie wants to be different. Look and write.

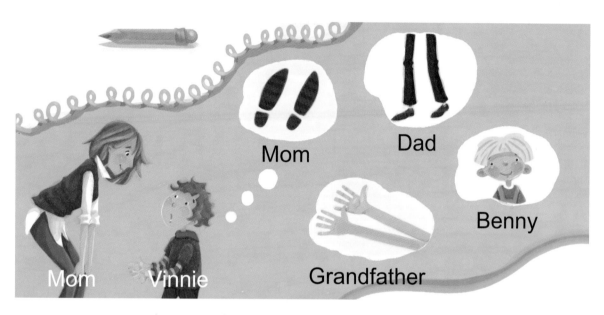

1. I want two big _____feet_____ like Mom.

2. I want long _____s like Dad.

3. I want straight _____ like Benny.

4. I want long _____s like Grandfather.

B Write Right!

Unscramble and write.

| like | I | long | Dad. | legs | want |

I _____ .

6. Clothes

A Words to Know

Highlight the words you know.

Target Words

clothes	coat	dress	jacket
jeans	pants	sweater	T-shirt
glasses	gloves	mittens	socks
shoes	boots	sandals	sneakers

B Clothes Line

See what's hanging on the line. Read and circle.

I see pants, jacket, coat, socks, and mittens.

C Letter to Letter

Look at the scattered letters. Connect and write.

1.

b	o	i	t	s
s	h	o	r	t

b				s
		boots		

2.

g	l	c	v	e	z
j	a	o	k	s	t

3.

g	l	e	a	t	e	t
s	w	a	s	s	b	s

D Laundry Day

Put the items in the right place. Find and write.

1. CLOTHES

_____ _____

_____ _____

2. SHOES

_____ _____

_____ _____

Word Bank

boots	shoes	dress	jeans
sandals	sneakers	sweater	T-shirt

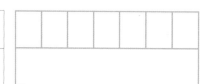

E Spilled Ink

Find the missing letters and solve the quiz.

1. c othes
   g asses
   sanda s

    is letter ☐ .

2. bo ts
   c at
   sh es
   s cks

    is letter ☐ .

3. sneacker
   kirt
   hirt
   pant

    is letter ☐ .

4. jack t
   dr ss
   glov s
   j ans

    is letter ☐ .

I want to wear my pink b____ ____u____ ____!

Words in Use

I want to wear my green T-shirt **and blue** pants.
I want to wear my dress **with my red** shoes.

 A **Emily's Outfit**

What does Emily want to wear? Look and circle.

1.

a. I want to wear my pink T-shirt and blue skirt.

b. I want to wear my green T-shirt and blue pants.

2.

a. I want to wear my dress with my red shoes.

b. I want to wear my jacket with my green sneakers.

B **How About You?**

What do you want to wear?

I want to wear _____.

A My Clothes

Look at the clothes on the floor. Look, circle, and write.

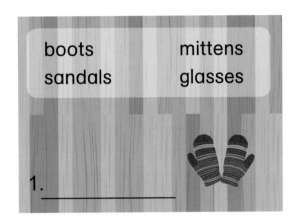

boots   mittens
sandals   glasses

1. _____

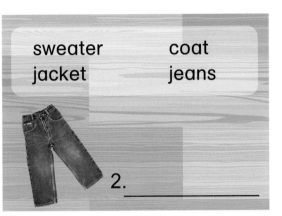

sweater   coat
jacket   jeans

2. _____

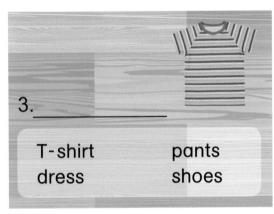

3. _____

T-shirt   pants
dress   shoes

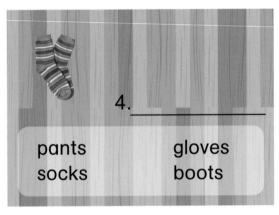

4. _____

pants   gloves
socks   boots

B Odd One Out

Find the different word. Read and circle.

1.   arm   hand   shoulder   pants

2.   neck   smell   see   hear

3.   sandals   sweater   sneakers   boots

4.   hair   face   clothes   mouth

Day 5

C Whatever You Wish

Read *Robert and Robot*. Look and write.

1.

"Robot, I want to dance."
"Yes, Robert. My fast ___feet___ will show you how to dance."

2.

"Robot, I want to play with the moon."
"Yes, Robert. My long _____s will bring you the moon."

3.

"Robot, I want to eat something sweet!"
"Yes, Robert. My quick _____s will bring you a chocolate cake."

4.

"Robot, I want to go home."
"Yes, Robert. My long _____s will carry you home."

7. Characteristics

A Words to Know

Highlight the words you know.

Target Words

brave	clever	creative	curious
foolish	funny	gentle	greedy
honest	independent	kind	lazy
mean	polite	shy	sweet

B Photo Album

Look at the pictures. Look and write.

1. _ _ y

2. f _ _ _ _

3. p _ _ _ _ _

4. gr _ _ d _

5. _ _ ri _ _ _

6. _ _ _ _ tive

C Story Pictures

Guess their characteristics. Look and circle.

1.

curious

lazy

foolish

2.

shy

funny

brave

3.

polite

greedy

creative

4.

mean

lazy

kind

D Dim Theater

See the words on the screen. Look and count.

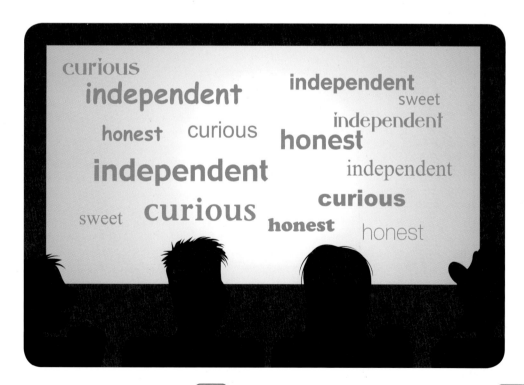

1. sweet ☐

2. curious ☐

3. independent ☐

4. honest ☐

E My Friends

Look at your friends! Find and write.

1.

   Kate and Amy are so _____.
   They make people laugh.

2. Adam is _____.
   He is the smartest in his class.

3. Bill is so _____.
   He does things on his own.

4. Jenny is quiet and _____.
   She doesn't like to speak in public.

5. Sam is _____.
   He wants to know everything.

Word Bank

shy   independent   curious   funny   clever

She is brave.

 A ## The King's Wife

The king is looking for a wife. Read and choose.

"I need a wife who is | brave | foolish |," said the king.

"There is a girl. She is | shy | brave |. Maybe she will look

into the mirror," said the barber.

"Wonderful! Ask her to come to my palace,"

said the king.

 B ## Read Again!

What is the girl like?

8. Jobs

A Words to Know

Highlight the words you know.

Target Words

jobs	artist	astronaut	baker	cook
dentist	designer	detective	doctor	engineer
farmer	pilot	reporter	scientist	singer
soldier	teacher	writer	police officer	

B Different People, Different Jobs!

Meet the people. Read and circle.

I see a cook, a singer, a doctor, an engineer, a farmer, a reporter, and an artist.

C Job Puzzle

Guess the jobs as a reporter. Match and trace.

1.

baker

2.

dentist

pilot

3.

soldier

4.

farmer

5.

artist

6.

detective

7.

singer

8.

astronaut

9.

police officer

10.

D Picture Code

Break the code to find the jobs. Find, write, and match.

c = ⬭	d = △	e = □	i = ▪
a = ⬭	o = ⬠	p = ⬡	r = ✚
h = ♥	t = ◆	w = ★	l = ☾

1. ⬡ ▪ ☾ ⬠ ◆

___ ___ ___ ___ ___

a

2. △ ⬠ ⬭ ◆ ⬠ ✚

___ ___ ___ ___ ___ ___

b

3. ★ ✚ ▪ ◆ □ ✚

___ ___ ___ ___ ___ ___

c

4. ◆ □ ⬭ ⬭ ♥ □ ✚

___ ___ ___ ___ ___ ___ ___

d

5. ✚ □ ⬡ ⬠ ✚ ◆ □ ✚

___ ___ ___ ___ ___ ___ ___ ___

e

Day 4

I want to be a designer!

 A **Career Day**

Today is Career Day. Look, find, and write.

1.

I want to be an
___architect___.

2.

I want to be a
_____.

3.

I want to be a
_____.

4.

I want to be a
_____.

Word Bank

architect	designer
teacher	reporter

 B **How About You?**

What do you want to be?

I want to be _____.

A People at Work

Make job titles. Complete the chart.

1. sing

2. report

3. farm

4. teach

5. write

6. bake

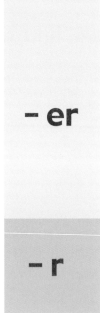

+

- er

- r

=

_____

_____

_____

_____

_____

_____

B Angry Letters

Calm down the letters. Unscramble and write in lowercase.

1. ZALY | | z |

2. MNAE | e | |

3. WESET   s | | | |

4. GETELN | | t | e |

5. RYGDEE | | d | |

6. LIFOOHS   f | | l | | |

C My Family

Read about Matt's family. Find and write.

My dad is a _____.
                  1

He is very _____. My mom is a s_____.
             2   3

She is really smart and c_____. My big sister is
                          4

an _____. She is good at painting. She is very
         5

_____. When I grow up, I want to be
       6

an _____. I am _____ about the universe.
       7   8

Word Bank

astronaut	clever	scientist	curious
brave	creative	police officer	artist

A Sentence Puzzle

Connect each sentence to the right answer. Match and trace.

1. What does Bobby see in the box? •

• a Go get a cow and a horse.

2. Is this a puzzle? •

• b He sees a circle this time.

3. What should I do? •

• c Yes, this is an animal puzzle.

B Wright Right!

Unscramble and write.

1. a star.　He　peeks inside　and sees

_____

2. Go get　a horse.　and　a cow

_____

3. monkey!　the funny　Look at

_____

4. elephant!　Look at　huge　the

_____

C Bookshelf

Put the missing books back. Find and write.

1. I want long _____ like Dad.

2. I want to wear my green T-shirt and blue_____ .

3. I want to wear my _____ with my red shoes.

4. She is _____ and clever.

5. I want to be a fashion _____!

Word Bank

legs   brave   dress   designer   pants

1. Shapes

p.2

B 1. rectangle 2. star 3. square
4. triangle 5. circle 6. oval
7. pentagon

p.3

C 1. star 2. triangle 3. circle
4. square 5. diamond 6. rectangle
D 1.cylinder 2. hexagon
3. pentagon 4. cone

p.4

E cylinder → oval → star → line →
diamond → circle → pentagon →
cone

p.5

A 1. square 2. circle 3. star
4. rectangle
B He peeks inside and sees a star.

2. Toys

p.6

B 1. dice 2. robot 3. block 4. jump
rope 5. kite 6. doll

p.7

C 1. doll 2. marble
3. puzzle 4. dice 5. robot
6. card 7. checkers 8. kite
9. block 10. slingshot

p.8

D 1. robot 2. dice 3. clay
4. doll 5. checkers

p.9

A 1. Is this a puzzle? 2. Yes, it is.
B puzzle, Yes

Review (1, 2)

p.10

A 1. **3** 2. **4** 3. **2** 4. **1** 5. **1**
B 1. cloudy, clay 2. rice, dice
3. bald, block

p.11

C 1. shapes 2. circle 3. block, doll

3. Farm Animals

p.12

B 1. rooster 2. horse 3. duck 4. cow
5. pig 6. sheep 7. rabbit

p.13

C 1. frog, b 2. sheep, f 3. pig, d
4. duck, c 5. dog, a 6. rooster, e
D hen, horse, goat

p.14

E 1. cat 2. pig 3. goat 4. hen
5. rooster 6. rabbit

p.15

A cow, horse
B Go get a cow and a horse.

4. Zoo Animals

p.16

B 1. bear 2. zebra 3. lion 4.giraffe
5. turtle 6. snake 7. elephant

p.17

C 1. bear 2. deer 3. tiger 4. snake
5. zebra 6. whale

p.18

D 1. turtle 2. monkey 3. kangaroo
4. giraffe 5. elephant 6. owl

p.19

A 1. the huge elephant
2. the funny monkey
B Look at the huge elephant!

Review (3, 4)

p.20

A 1. sheep / duck / rabbit / cow
2. tiger / bear / fox / giraffe
B 1. rabbit 2. wolf 3. cat

p.21

C 1. a 2. d 3. b 4. c

5. Body Parts

p.22

B 1. eye 2. nose 3. ear 4. leg
5. foot 6. arm 7. mouth 8. shoulder

p.23

C 1. see, **b** eye 2. smell, **d** nose
3. hear, **a** ear 4. feel, **c** hand
D 1. face 2. neck 3. finger 4. mouth
5. shoulder

p.24

E

1. mouth 2. head 3. foot 4. leg
5. finger 6. nose 7. arm 8. hair

p.25

A 1. feet 2. leg 3. hair 4. arm
B I want long legs like Dad.

6. Clothes

p.26

B

p.27

C 1. boots 2. jacket 3. glasses
D 1. dress, jeans, sweater, T-shirt
2. boots, shoes, sandals, sneakers

p.28

E 1. l 2. o 3. s 4. e / blouse

p.29

A 1. b 2. a

Review (5, 6)

p.30

A 1. mittens 2. jeans 3. T-shirt
4. socks
B 1. pants 2. neck 3. sweater
4. clothes

p.31

C 1. feet 2. arm 3. hand 4. leg

7. Characteristics

p.32

B 1. shy 2. funny 3. polite 4. greedy
5. curious 6. creative

p.33

C 1. curious 2. brave 3. greedy
4. kind
D 1. **2** 2. **4** 3. **5** 4. **4**

p.34

E 1. funny 2. clever 3. independent
4. shy 5. curious

p.35

A brave, brave
B She is brave.

8. Jobs

p.36

B

p.37

C 1. pilot 2. dentist 3. baker
4. artist 5. detective 6. soldier
7. police officer 8. farmer
9. astronaut 10. singer

p.38

E 1. pilot, c 2. doctor, d
3. writer, a 4. teacher, e 5. reporter, b

p.39

A 1. architect 2. teacher 3. designer
4. reporter

Review (7, 8)

p.40

A 1. singer 2. reporter 3. farmer
4. teacher 5. writer 6. baker
B 1. lazy 2. mean 3. sweet 4. gentle
5. greedy 6. foolish

p.41

C 1. police officer 2. brave
3. scientist 4. clever 5. artist
6. creative 7. astronaut 8. curious

Expressions Review

p.42

A 1. b 2. c 3. a
B 1. He peeks inside and sees a
star.
2. Go get a cow and a horse.
3. Look at the funny monkey!
4. Look at the huge elephant!

p.43

C 1. legs 2. pants 3. dress 4. brave
5. designer

Shapes

shapes

Shapes

square

Shapes

rectangle

Shapes

triangle

Shapes

circle

Shapes

oval

Shapes

star

Shapes

line

Shapes

pentagon

Shapes

hexagon

Shapes

cone

Shapes

diamond

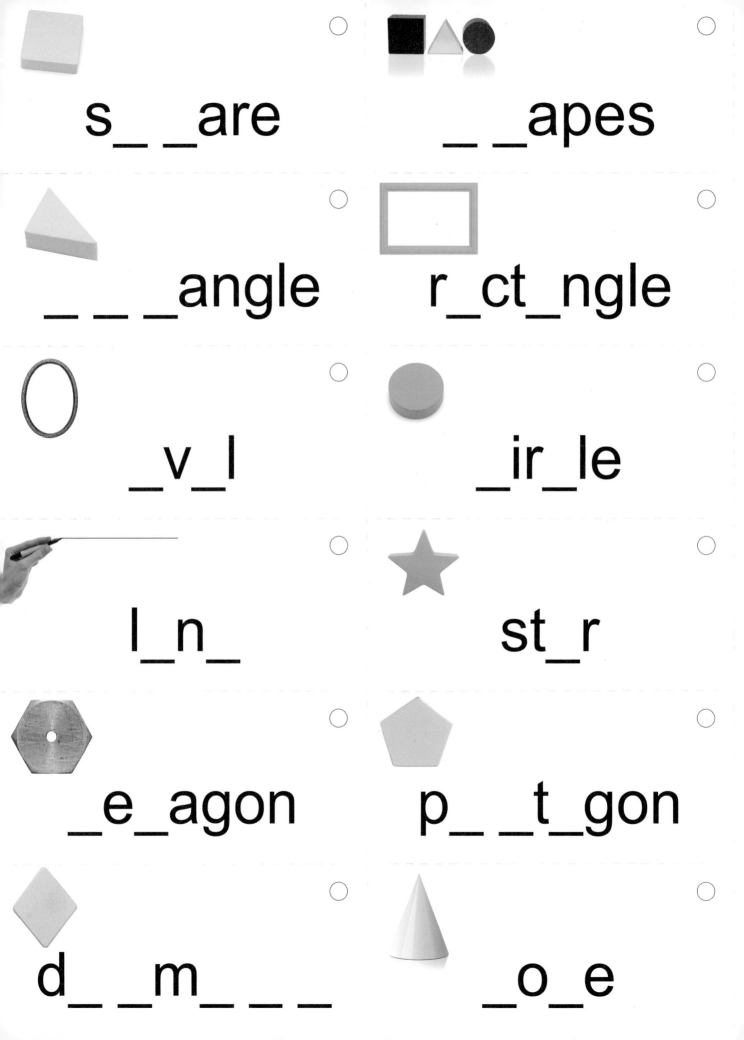

s_ _ are

_ _ apes

_ _ _angle

r_ct_ngle

_v_l

_ir_le

l_n_

st_r

_e_agon

p_ _ _t_gon

d_ _ _m_ _ _ _

_o_e

toys

block

card

puzzle

kite

doll

dice

jump rope

robot

checkers

clay

marble

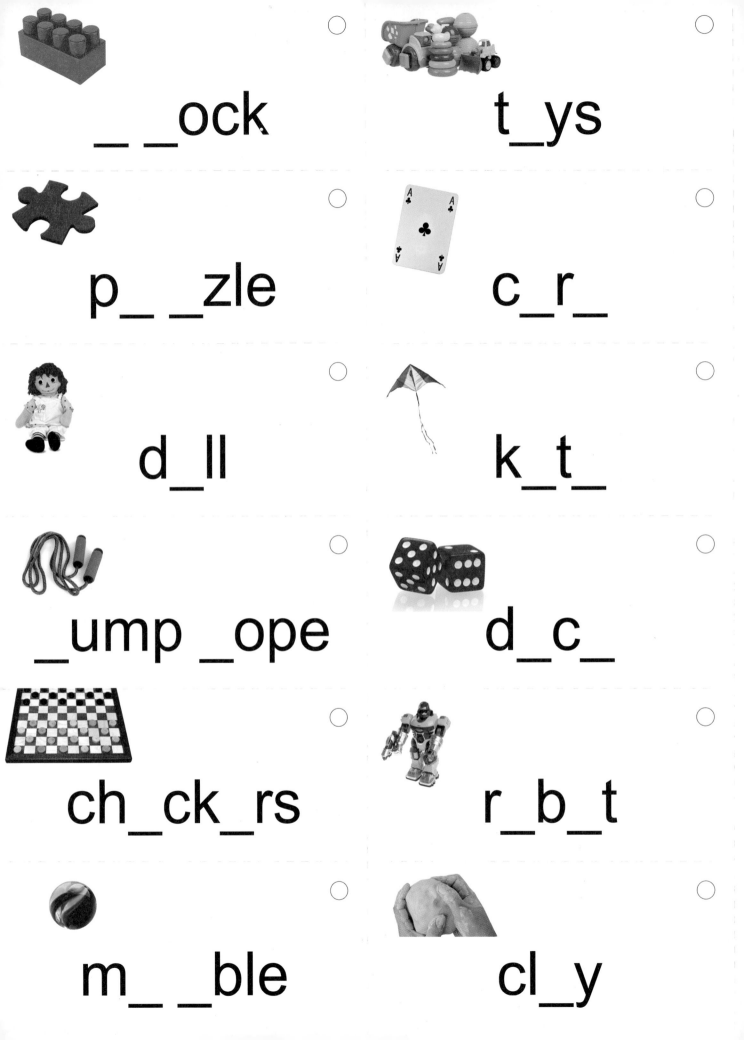

_ _ock

t_ys

p_ _zle

c_r_

d_ll

k_t_

_ump _ope

d_c_

ch_ck_rs

r_b_t

m_ _ble

cl_y

farm animals

hen

rooster

cat

frog

goat

horse

pig

rabbit

sheep

duck

cow

h_n

f_ _m animals

c_t

r_ _ster

g_ _t

f_ _g

p_g

h_ _se

_ _eep

r_bb_t

c_w

d_ck

zoo animals

bear

snake

zebra

lion

elephant

tiger

dolphin

giraffe

wolf

turtle

kangaroo

b _ _ r

z _ _ animals

_ eb _ a

sn _ k _

ele _ _ ant

l _ _ n

dol _ _ in

t _ g _ r

w _ _ f

g _ r _ ff _

k _ ng _ r _ _

t _ r _ le

body

head

face

eye

nose

mouth

neck

shoulder

arm

hand

finger

leg

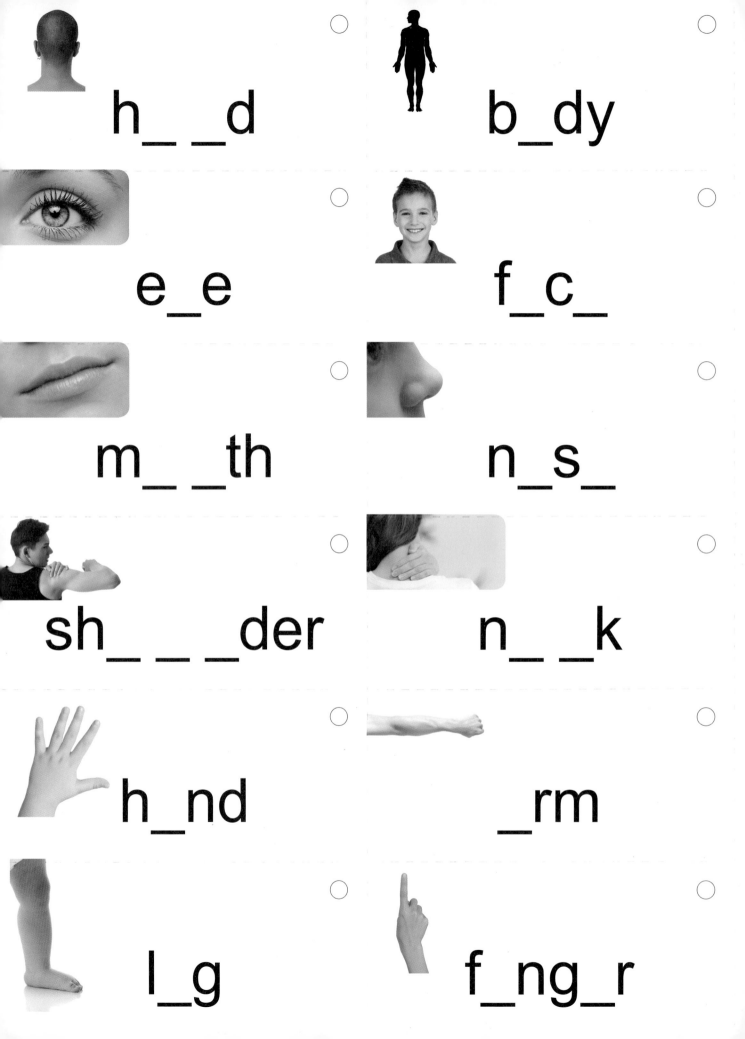

h _ _ d

b _ dy

e _ e

f _ c _

m _ _ th

n _ s _

sh _ _ _ der

n _ _ k

h _ nd

_ rm

l _ g

f _ ng _ r

clothes

coat

dress

T-shirt

jacket

pants

socks

sweater

glasses

shoes

sneakers

gloves

c_ _t

clo_ _es

T-sh_rt

dr_s_

p_nt_

j_ck_t

sw_ _ter

s_ck_

sh_ _s

glass_ _

_ _oves

_ _eakers

kind

sweet

funny

curious

brave

honest

clever

shy

lazy

polite

independent

creative

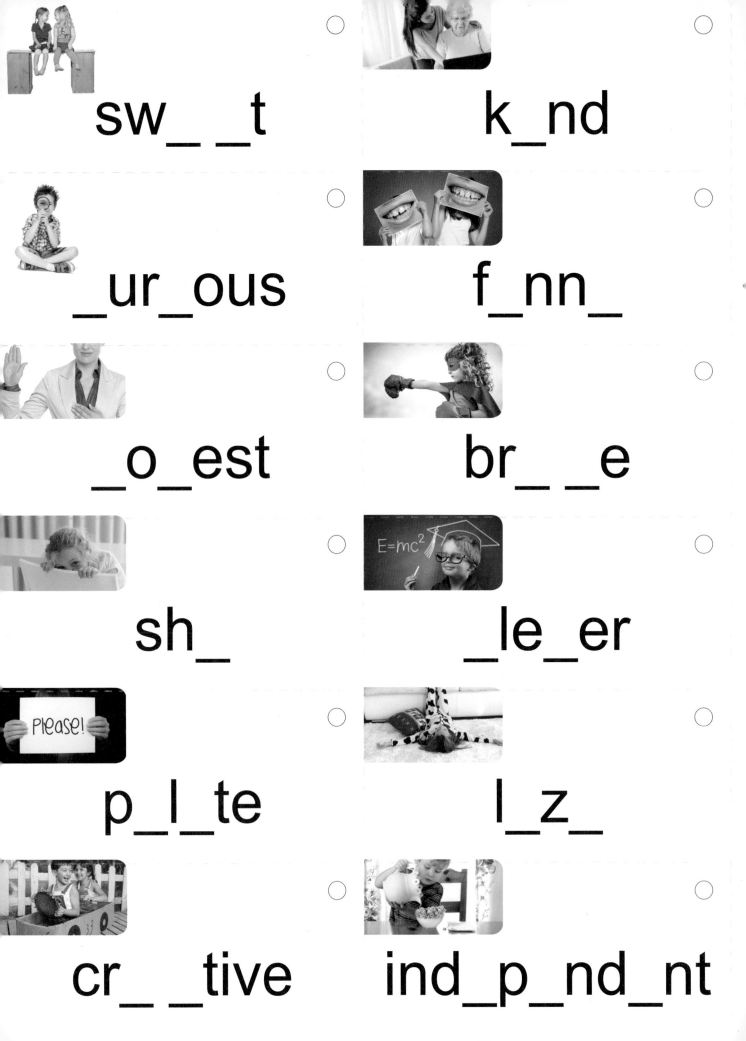

sw_ _t

k_nd

_ur_ous

f_nn_

_o_est

br_ _e

sh_

_le_er

p_l_te

l_z_

cr_ _tive

ind_p_nd_nt

Jobs	Jobs
teacher	scientist
Jobs	Jobs
doctor	farmer
Jobs	Jobs
soldier	cook
Jobs	Jobs
baker	dentist
Jobs	Jobs
police officer	singer
Jobs	Jobs
artist	engineer

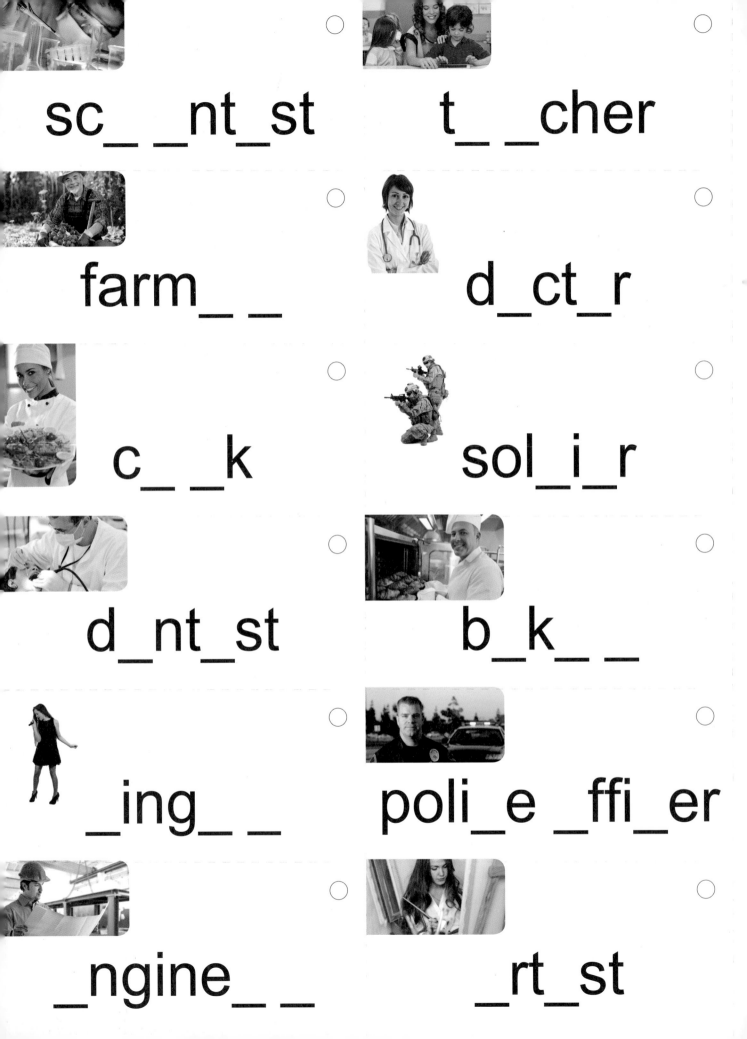

sc_ _nt_st

t_ _cher

farm_ _

d_ct_r

c_ _k

sol_i_r

d_nt_st

b_k_ _

ing _

poli_e _ffi_er

ngine _

_rt_st